Wealth Mindset: Unleashing Financial Freedom with Rich Dad's Wisdom

Introduction

Welcome to "Wealth Mindset: Unleashing Financial Freedom with Rich Dad's Wisdom." In the pages that follow, we embark on a journey of empowerment, enlightenment, and transformation—a journey towards unlocking the secrets to lasting wealth, abundance, and financial freedom.

In a world where financial literacy is often overlooked, and the path to prosperity seems elusive for many, this book serves as a guiding light, illuminating the principles and practices that lead to financial success. Drawing inspiration from the timeless wisdom of Robert T. Kiyosaki's "Rich Dad Poor Dad," we explore the fundamental truths about money, mindset, and wealth-building that have the power to change lives and reshape destinies.

Throughout these pages, you will discover the importance of financial education, the power of passive income, the mindset shifts needed to overcome limiting beliefs, and the actionable steps you can take to achieve your financial goals. From understanding the difference between assets and liabilities to embracing entrepreneurship, from setting clear financial goals to taking decisive action towards achieving them, each chapter is designed to empower you with the knowledge, tools, and inspiration needed to create a life of abundance and prosperity.

But this book is more than just a manual for financial success—it is a call to action, a manifesto for personal empowerment, and a testament to the boundless potential that lies within each of us. As you embark on this journey, I invite you to approach it with an open mind, a willingness to learn, and a commitment to taking bold, decisive action towards your financial dreams.

So, let us embark on this journey together, as we unlock the secrets to financial freedom, embrace the abundance mindset, and create a future of unlimited possibility and prosperity. The power to change your financial destiny lies within your hands—let us begin.

Content

Chapter 1
The Power of Financial Education

In the journey towards financial freedom, education is the cornerstone upon which success is built. Yet, despite the emphasis on education in our society, the subject of personal finance is often neglected in traditional schooling. This chapter explores the vital role of financial education in achieving lasting wealth and prosperity.

Financial literacy encompasses the knowledge and skills necessary to make informed decisions about money management, investing, and wealth-building. It goes beyond basic math skills and encompasses concepts such as budgeting, saving, investing, and debt management. However, many individuals lack even the most fundamental understanding of these concepts, leaving them vulnerable to financial pitfalls and setbacks.

Without a solid foundation in financial education, individuals may find themselves trapped in a cycle of debt, living paycheck to paycheck, and unable to build wealth for the future. They may fall victim to predatory lending practices, make uninformed investment decisions, or struggle to navigate complex financial systems. In contrast, those who prioritize financial education are better equipped to make wise financial choices, grow their wealth, and achieve financial independence.

Financial education empowers individuals to take control of their financial destinies, providing them with the tools and knowledge needed to make sound financial decisions. It enables individuals to budget effectively, manage debt responsibly, invest wisely, and plan for the future with confidence. By investing in their financial education, individuals can break free from the constraints of financial insecurity and create a life of abundance and prosperity.

In today's rapidly evolving financial landscape, the importance of financial education cannot be overstated. By prioritizing financial literacy and seeking out opportunities for learning and growth, individuals can unlock the door to financial freedom and build a secure future for themselves and their loved ones. This chapter serves as a call to action, urging readers to embrace the power of financial education and embark on their journey towards wealth and prosperity.

Chapter 2
Contrasting Mindsets: Rich Dad vs. Poor Dad

In "Rich Dad Poor Dad," Robert T. Kiyosaki introduces readers to the contrasting mindsets of his two influential father figures: his biological father, whom he refers to as "poor dad," and his best friend's father, whom he calls "rich dad." This chapter delves into the profound impact of these two distinct perspectives on money and wealth, shaping Kiyosaki's own understanding and approach to financial success.

Kiyosaki's poor dad epitomized the conventional mindset towards money—a mindset rooted in fear, scarcity, and a reliance on traditional paths to financial security. Poor dad believed in the importance of education and hard work but viewed a stable job with benefits as the ultimate goal. He cautioned against taking risks and encouraged his son to follow a safe, predictable career path.

In stark contrast, Kiyosaki's rich dad embodied a radically different mindset—one characterized by entrepreneurial spirit, innovation, and a willingness to take calculated risks. Rich dad understood the power of financial education and believed in leveraging assets to generate passive income. He encouraged Kiyosaki to think creatively, challenge the status quo, and pursue opportunities for wealth creation outside the confines of traditional employment.

Through his interactions with both father figures, Kiyosaki gleaned invaluable insights into the principles of wealth-building and success. He learned that mindset plays a crucial role in determining one's financial destiny and that embracing a mindset of abundance and possibility opens the door to unlimited opportunities. Rich dad taught Kiyosaki the importance of financial independence, asset accumulation, and investing in oneself through continuous learning and personal development.

This chapter prompts readers to reflect on their own mindset towards money and wealth, encouraging them to identify any limiting beliefs or misconceptions that may be holding them back from achieving their financial goals. By recognizing the influence of their upbringing and experiences on their financial mindset, readers can begin to adopt the empowering principles espoused by rich dad and cultivate a mindset of abundance, resourcefulness, and financial freedom.

The contrasting mindsets of rich dad and poor dad serve as a powerful reminder that financial success is not solely determined by external circumstances but by one's beliefs, attitudes, and actions. By embracing the mindset of rich dad and adopting a proactive, entrepreneurial approach to wealth-building, readers can transcend the limitations of conventional thinking and unlock their full potential for financial abundance and prosperity.

Chapter 3
Assets vs. Liabilities: Building Wealth Brick by Brick

In the pursuit of financial freedom, understanding the difference between assets and liabilities is paramount. This chapter explores the fundamental concepts of assets and liabilities and their profound implications for wealth creation and financial stability.

An asset is anything that puts money in your pocket, while a liability is anything that takes money out of your pocket. Assets have the potential to generate income and appreciate in value over time, such as real estate, stocks, bonds, and businesses. Liabilities, on the other hand, represent financial obligations and expenses, such as mortgages, car loans, credit card debt, and living expenses.

Assets are the building blocks of wealth—they provide opportunities for passive income, capital appreciation, and financial security. By accumulating income-generating assets, individuals can create a steady stream of passive income that exceeds their expenses, allowing them to achieve financial independence and freedom. Examples of assets include rental properties that generate rental income, dividend-paying stocks that provide regular cash flow, and business ventures that yield profits.

While liabilities are an inevitable part of life, minimizing unnecessary liabilities can help individuals preserve their wealth and financial resources. This may involve reducing consumer debt, avoiding high-interest loans, and living below one's means. By prioritizing the acquisition of assets over liabilities, individuals can gradually shift their financial trajectory towards prosperity and abundance.

Cash flow—the movement of money in and out of one's financial portfolio—is a crucial indicator of financial health and stability. Positive cash flow, generated from income-producing assets, enables individuals to cover expenses, reinvest in their assets, and build wealth over time. By focusing on building positive cash flow through strategic asset allocation and investment decisions, individuals can create a solid foundation for long-term financial success.

This chapter concludes by outlining practical strategies for building wealth through asset accumulation and liability management. These strategies include diversifying investments, leveraging other people's money (OPM) to finance asset purchases, and continually educating oneself about investment opportunities and financial markets.

In the journey towards financial freedom, mastering the principles of asset accumulation and liability management is essential. By prioritizing the acquisition of income-generating assets and minimizing unnecessary liabilities, individuals can lay the groundwork for lasting wealth and prosperity. This chapter serves as a blueprint for
building wealth brick by brick, empowering readers to take control of their financial future and achieve their dreams of abundance and financial freedom.

Chapter 4
Harnessing the Power of Passive Income

Passive income is the holy grail of financial independence—it is the income earned with minimal effort or active involvement, allowing individuals to generate wealth and achieve freedom from the constraints of traditional employment. This chapter delves into the concept of passive income, its various sources, and the transformative impact it can have on one's financial well-being.

Passive income is income earned from investments, businesses, or other ventures in which the individual is not actively involved on a day-to-day basis. Unlike active income, which requires continuous effort and time, passive income flows in consistently, providing a steady stream of revenue even when one is not actively working. Examples of passive income sources include rental income from real estate properties, dividends from stocks, royalties from intellectual property, and interest from savings accounts or bonds.

Passive income offers numerous advantages over traditional forms of income, including flexibility, scalability, and the potential for exponential growth. By diversifying income streams and leveraging passive income sources, individuals can achieve financial independence, retire early, and pursue their passions and interests without being tied to a traditional job. Passive income also provides a safety net during economic downturns or unexpected life events, offering stability and peace of mind in uncertain times.

Building passive income streams requires careful planning, strategic investment, and a willingness to take calculated risks. This may involve investing in income-producing assets such as rental properties, dividend-paying stocks, or peer-to-peer lending platforms. It may also entail starting a side business or creating digital products and services that generate recurring revenue. By consistently reinvesting profits and compounding returns over time, individuals can accelerate the growth of their passive income streams and achieve financial freedom faster.

Passive income plays a crucial role in achieving financial goals and building long-term wealth. It provides a reliable source of income that is not contingent on the number of hours worked or the performance of the economy. By incorporating passive income into their financial plans, individuals can create a sustainable income stream that supports their desired lifestyle and allows them to pursue their dreams without financial constraints.

Passive income is a powerful tool for achieving financial independence and unlocking the door to limitless opportunities. By harnessing the power of passive income, individuals can break free from the limitations of traditional employment, build wealth on their own terms, and live life on their own terms. This chapter serves as a guide to understanding passive income, identifying opportunities for generating passive income, and taking actionable steps towards financial freedom and abundance.

Chapter 5
Striving for Financial Independence

Financial independence is the ultimate goal for many individuals—it is the state of being where one's passive income exceeds their expenses, providing the freedom to live life on their own terms without being reliant on a paycheck. This chapter explores the concept of financial independence, its significance in achieving lasting wealth, and the steps individuals can take to strive towards this coveted goal.

Financial independence is the state of having enough income from passive sources to cover all living expenses without the need for active employment. It represents the ultimate form of financial freedom, where individuals have the flexibility to pursue their passions, travel the world, or spend time with loved ones without worrying about money. Achieving financial independence requires careful planning, disciplined saving, and strategic investment in income-generating assets.

The journey towards financial independence begins with setting clear financial goals and creating a roadmap for achieving them. This may involve calculating one's financial independence number—the amount of passive income required to cover all living expenses—and identifying strategies for accumulating sufficient assets to generate this income. It also requires adopting a frugal mindset, prioritizing savings over consumption, and making deliberate choices that align with long-term financial objectives.

Passive income plays a central role in achieving financial independence—it is the key to generating ongoing cash flow that sustains one's desired lifestyle without the need for active work. By building multiple streams of passive income through investments, businesses, or other ventures, individuals can diversify their income sources and create a stable foundation for financial independence. Passive income provides a safety net during economic downturns or job loss, ensuring continued financial security and peace of mind.

There are various strategies individuals can employ to accelerate their journey towards financial independence. These may include increasing income through career advancement, entrepreneurship, or side hustles, reducing expenses through frugal living and smart budgeting, and maximizing investment returns through asset allocation and tax-efficient strategies. By continually optimizing their financial plan and staying disciplined in their approach, individuals can expedite their path to financial independence and achieve their goals sooner.

While the pursuit of financial independence requires discipline and sacrifice, it is essential to celebrate milestones along the way and enjoy the journey. Whether it's reaching a savings goal, achieving a certain level of passive income, or experiencing the freedom to pursue new opportunities, each step forward brings individuals closer to their vision of financial independence. By embracing the process and staying focused on their long-term goals, individuals can create a life of abundance, fulfillment, and financial freedom.

Financial independence is not merely a destination but a journey—a journey of self-discovery, empowerment, and fulfillment. By embracing the principles of financial independence and taking actionable steps towards their goals, individuals can create a future of unlimited possibilities and live life on their own terms. This chapter serves as a roadmap for navigating the path to financial independence, empowering readers to take control of their financial future and achieve lasting prosperity and freedom.

Chapter 6
Embracing Entrepreneurship: Creating Your Path to Wealth

Entrepreneurship is a powerful vehicle for wealth creation—it offers individuals the opportunity to build successful businesses, generate passive income, and achieve financial freedom on their own terms. This chapter explores the transformative potential of entrepreneurship, the mindset and skills required for success, and practical steps individuals can take to embark on their entrepreneurial journey.

At its core, entrepreneurship is about embracing a mindset of innovation, creativity, and resourcefulness. It requires a willingness to take risks, overcome challenges, and seize opportunities in the pursuit of one's vision. Successful entrepreneurs possess traits such as resilience, adaptability, and a relentless drive to succeed. They are not deterred by failure but view it as a valuable learning experience on the path to success.

Entrepreneurship is about identifying unmet needs, solving problems, and creating value for others. This may involve developing innovative products or services, disrupting existing industries, or capitalizing on emerging trends and market gaps. Successful entrepreneurs have a keen eye for opportunity and are adept at recognizing and capitalizing on untapped markets or underserved niches.

Turning entrepreneurial ideas into reality requires careful planning, strategic execution, and a willingness to take decisive action. This may involve conducting market research, validating product-market fit, developing a business plan, and securing funding or resources to launch and grow the business. Whether starting a small side hustle or scaling a full-fledged startup, the key is to take consistent, focused action towards achieving your entrepreneurial goals.

Entrepreneurship is not without its challenges—it requires resilience, perseverance, and a willingness to pivot in the face of adversity. From funding constraints and market competition to operational hurdles and unforeseen setbacks, entrepreneurs must navigate a myriad of obstacles on their journey to success. However, it is often these challenges that spur innovation, foster growth, and ultimately lead to greater achievements in the long run.

As entrepreneurs grow their ventures, they must also focus on scaling their operations, optimizing efficiency, and sustaining long-term growth. This may involve expanding into new markets, diversifying revenue streams, building a strong team, and fostering a culture of innovation and continuous improvement. By staying agile, adaptable, and customer-focused, entrepreneurs can position their businesses for sustainable success in an ever-changing marketplace.

Entrepreneurship is not just about building businesses—it's about creating opportunities, making an impact, and shaping the future. By embracing the entrepreneurial mindset and taking bold, decisive action, individuals can unleash their full potential, achieve financial independence, and leave a lasting legacy. This chapter serves as a call to action for aspiring entrepreneurs, urging them to seize the opportunities before them, pursue their passions with purpose, and embark on a journey of limitless possibility and potential.

Chapter 7
Taking Action: The Key to Unlocking Financial Success

Action is the catalyst for change—it is the force that propels individuals forward on their journey towards financial success and abundance. This chapter explores the importance of taking action, overcoming fear and procrastination, and cultivating the habits and mindset needed to achieve one's financial goals.

Many individuals dream of financial success but are held back by fear, self-doubt, and inertia. They may procrastinate, make excuses, or succumb to analysis paralysis, preventing them from taking the necessary steps towards their goals. However, without action, dreams remain just that—mere fantasies that never materialize into reality.

Fear of failure, fear of rejection, fear of the unknown—these are common obstacles that stand in the way of taking action. However, it is often through confronting and overcoming these fears that individuals experience personal growth and achieve breakthroughs in their lives. By reframing failure as a learning opportunity, embracing uncertainty as a catalyst for growth, and cultivating a mindset of resilience and determination, individuals can overcome their fears and take bold, decisive action towards their goals.

Action begins with clarity of purpose and direction. Setting specific, measurable, achievable, relevant, and time-bound (SMART) goals provides a roadmap for success and helps individuals stay focused and motivated. Breaking down goals into smaller, actionable steps makes them more manageable and reduces overwhelm, making it easier to take consistent action towards achieving them.

Success is not a one-time event but the culmination of daily habits and routines. By cultivating habits that support their goals—such as disciplined saving, continuous learning, and proactive problem-solving—individuals can create a foundation for long-term success and resilience. Habits such as goal-setting, time management, and self-discipline are essential for overcoming inertia and maintaining momentum on the path to financial success.

Accountability and support play a crucial role in sustaining motivation and momentum. Whether through accountability partners, mentors, or support networks, having others hold you to your commitments and provide encouragement and guidance can make all the difference in staying on track towards your goals. Surrounding yourself with like-minded individuals who share your vision and values can also provide inspiration, motivation, and a sense of community on the journey towards financial success.

Taking action is not just about achieving the end result—it's about embracing the process, celebrating progress, and learning from setbacks along the way. Each step forward, no matter how small, brings individuals closer to their goals and reinforces their confidence and belief in their ability to succeed. By adopting a growth mindset, viewing challenges as opportunities, and staying resilient in the face of adversity, individuals can overcome obstacles and continue moving forward on their path to financial success.

Action is the bridge between dreams and reality—it is the key to unlocking the door to financial success and abundance. By overcoming fear, setting clear goals, developing empowering habits, and seeking support and accountability, individuals can take control of their financial future and create a life of unlimited possibility and potential. This chapter serves as a reminder that the power to change lies within each of us—and that the journey to financial success begins with taking the first step forward.

Chapter 8
Shifting Perspectives: Rethinking Money and Wealth

The way we think about money and wealth shapes our beliefs, attitudes, and behaviors towards financial success. In this final chapter, we explore the importance of shifting perspectives, challenging limiting beliefs, and adopting empowering mindsets that pave the way for abundance, prosperity, and fulfillment.

Society often perpetuates certain myths and misconceptions about money and wealth—such as the belief that wealth is reserved for the lucky or privileged few, or that financial success requires sacrificing happiness or integrity. However, these limiting beliefs only serve to reinforce scarcity and hold individuals back from realizing their full potential. By questioning conventional wisdom and challenging limiting beliefs, individuals can open themselves up to new possibilities and opportunities for growth and prosperity.

At the core of shifting perspectives is cultivating an abundance mindset—a belief in the inherent abundance of the universe and one's ability to attract and create wealth and opportunities. An abundance mindset is characterized by optimism, gratitude, and a focus on possibilities rather than limitations. It involves reframing setbacks as opportunities for growth, celebrating the success of others, and trusting in one's ability to overcome challenges and achieve their goals.

True wealth extends beyond monetary riches—it encompasses fulfillment, purpose, and a sense of meaning and contribution. By redefining success on their own terms and aligning their actions with their values and passions, individuals can create a life of fulfillment and abundance that transcends material wealth alone. Success is not measured by the size of one's bank account but by the impact one makes in the world and the fulfillment one experiences in their journey towards their goals.

As individuals achieve success and abundance, it is important to give back to others and contribute to the greater good. Whether through philanthropy, volunteering, or mentorship, giving back not only benefits those in need but also enriches the lives of the givers themselves. It fosters a sense of connection, purpose, and fulfillment, and reinforces the belief that true wealth is measured not by what one accumulates but by what one gives.

The journey towards financial success is a lifelong pursuit—one that requires continuous learning, growth, and adaptation to change. By remaining open-minded, curious, and committed to personal and professional development, individuals can stay ahead of the curve, seize new opportunities, and navigate the complexities of an ever-changing world. Lifelong learning not only expands one's knowledge and skills but also fosters creativity, resilience, and a sense of possibility and wonder.

Shifting perspectives is not a one-time event but an ongoing process of self-discovery, growth, and transformation. By challenging limiting beliefs, cultivating an abundance mindset, and aligning their actions with their values and passions, individuals can create a life of abundance, fulfillment, and purpose. This chapter serves as a reminder that true wealth lies not in what we have but in who we are—and that by embracing a mindset of abundance and possibility, we can unlock the limitless potential within ourselves and create a future of unlimited opportunity and prosperity.

Conclusion
Empowering You to Achieve Financial Freedom

In the pages of this book, we have embarked on a journey of discovery, empowerment, and transformation—a journey towards financial freedom and abundance. From understanding the power of financial education to embracing entrepreneurship, from harnessing the potential of passive income to shifting perspectives on money and wealth, each chapter has been a stepping stone towards realizing your full potential and unlocking the door to financial success.

As we reach the conclusion of this book, I want to leave you with a few key takeaways that encapsulate the essence of our exploration:

Knowledge is Power: Financial education is the foundation upon which financial success is built. By equipping yourself with the knowledge and skills needed to make informed decisions about money and investing, you empower yourself to take control of your financial future and create the life of abundance you desire.

Mindset Matters: Your mindset plays a critical role in shaping your financial destiny. By adopting an abundance mindset, cultivating resilience, and embracing the possibilities that surround you, you can overcome obstacles, seize opportunities, and achieve your goals with confidence and determination.

Action is Key: Success is not merely the result of wishful thinking or idle dreaming—it is the product of deliberate, focused action. By taking consistent, purposeful steps towards your goals, you move closer to realizing your vision of financial freedom and abundance.

Embrace Growth and Adaptation: The journey towards financial freedom is a dynamic, ever-evolving process. Embrace change, stay open to new opportunities, and continually seek out ways to learn, grow, and evolve as an individual.

Share Your Success: As you achieve success and abundance in your own life, remember to pay it forward and give back to others. Whether through acts of kindness, mentorship, or philanthropy, use your success as a platform for positive change and contribution to the greater good.

Ultimately, the path to financial freedom is not a destination but a journey—a journey of self-discovery, empowerment, and fulfillment. As you continue on your path, remember that you hold the power to create the life of abundance and prosperity you desire. Believe in yourself, trust in your abilities, and never lose sight of the limitless potential that lies within you.

Thank you for joining me on this journey. May you continue to thrive, grow, and achieve your dreams of financial freedom and abundance.

Acknowledgments

I would like to extend my heartfelt gratitude to everyone who has contributed to the creation of this book, "Wealth Mindset: Unleashing Financial Freedom with Rich Dad's Wisdom."

First and foremost, I am deeply grateful to Robert T. Kiyosaki, whose groundbreaking work in "Rich Dad Poor Dad" has inspired millions around the world to rethink their approach to money and wealth. Your wisdom, insights, and unwavering commitment to empowering others have laid the foundation for this book, and I am honored to build upon your legacy.

I would like to express my appreciation to my family and friends for their unwavering support and encouragement throughout this journey. I am also indebted to the countless mentors, teachers, and thought leaders whose guidance and mentorship have enriched my life and shaped my understanding of finance and entrepreneurship. Your wisdom and expertise have been invaluable in shaping the ideas presented in this book.

To my readers, I extend my deepest thanks for your interest in this book and your commitment to personal growth and financial empowerment. It is my sincere hope that the insights shared within these pages will empower you to take control of your financial future and create the life of abundance and prosperity you deserve.

Finally, I would like to thank the entire team at Twilight Ink Publishing, whose dedication, professionalism, and expertise have made this book a reality. Your hard work and collaboration have been instrumental in bringing this project to fruition.

Thank you to everyone who has contributed to this book in ways large and small. Your support and encouragement have made all the difference, and I am profoundly grateful for your contributions.

With deepest gratitude,

Chandni Inkwell